RIPPLE

The Ultimate Guide To The World Of Ripple

Ikuya Takashima

Copyright © 2018 Ikuya Takashima

All rights reserved.

ISBN:1986181618
ISBN-13:9781986181617

CONTENTS

Introduction i

Chapter One: History Of Ripple 1

Chapter Two: How Does Ripple Work? 15

Chapter Three: Ripple And Other Cryptocurrencies 22

Chapter Four: Investing In Ripple 35

Chapter Five: Areas Of Concern For Ripple 44

Chapter Six: Current Happenings In Ripple 52

Chapter Seven: The Future Of Cryptocurrency 59

Chapter Eight: Advice For Investing In Ripple 76

Final Words 89

Other Ikuya Takashima books available on Amazon 92

About The Author 93

Introduction

Turn on any news outlet or business channel today, or browse through financial news sites and publications, and you will inevitably see much discussion and speculation regarding cryptocurrency and how it is the future of currency, or how its latest bubble is about to burst. Investors, financial experts, and industry analysts all have their opinions on cryptocurrency and whether it is a sound investment. Some advise their followers to go all in and bet big on cryptocurrency while it is still on the rise, while others call for more caution and view cryptocurrency as a high-risk venture. Of course, there are those who avoid cryptocurrency at all, deeming virtual currency as a future failure with far-reaching consequences when it inevitably crashes.

Whether it is raved about or railed against, cryptocurrency has indeed become a worldwide phenomenon, capturing the attention and the avid interest of both casual and ardent investors alike. It is being adopted by banks and financial institutions eager to cater to a growing market of cryptocurrency investors, and many big-name companies have also capitulated to cryptocurrency as an accepted form of payment for goods and services. Some governments have also taken steps to integrate cryptocurrency in their services.

It is not hard to understand why cryptocurrency has become the darling of the financial world in such a rapid period of time. As the world has become connected online, the Internet has taken over much of daily life in one way or another. Many tasks or daily activities have transitioned to becoming online services, allowing users to complete their required tasks anywhere they are with Internet access and a Web-enabled device. Shopping, banking, communication, entertainment, and many other facets of modern life are now performed or processed online. As people have become used to their daily lives becoming more dependent on the Internet and the digital transfer of data, financial currency followed suit.

Banks and financial service providers were among the early adopters of the online revolution. As reliable Internet access became available to the general public, so did the popularity of online banking and Web-based financial transactions. Online banking services allowed users to skip the long lines at their local bank branches, as they were given the option of performing transactions such as fund transfers, bill payments, and account management at their fingertips.

Back in the 1980's and 1990's, there were already several attempts by inventors to produce a digital cash system or virtual currency. Online banking, while based online and available to anyone with Internet access, still relied on currencies backed by government reserves, and as such were still subject to government scrutiny. Also, state-backed currencies can be controlled or limited by central banks or authorities, and are also prone to external factors such as political upheaval, economic downturn, or devaluation.

Long before the concept of cryptocurrency as we know it today came into fruition, there were already trailblazers who saw the potential of electronic money and a currency that is 100% virtual, free from the control of any existing government oversight. One of the earliest iterations was conceptualized by David Chaum, a cryptographer, who designed an anonymous electronic money system in 1983. Dubbed as E-cash, this system used cryptography in electronic payment transactions. Years later, Chaum applied this cryptographic money system through the Digicash system, utilizing digital currency with key encryption and keeping the currency free from government or third-party monitoring.

Another anonymous electronic cash platform was conceptualized by Wei Dai in 1998 when he released his design of "B-money". Around this time, another electronic currency system, Bitgold, was created by Nick Szabo. Bitgold used a proof of work function and a cryptographic system for requiring users to complete transactions. The initial concepts of Szabo and Dai, which based the virtual currency on proof of work solutions would become the groundwork of many later cryptocurrencies.

The biggest and most widely known cryptocurrency today, Bitcoin, was launched in 2009 by Satoshi Nakamoto. Satoshi did not originally set out to invent a currency, but rather a peer-to-peer electronic cash system. His intention was to succeed in creating a digital cash platform that would be decentralized and self-sustaining, and would overcome the obstacles that other virtual cash systems could not hurdle in the past. Satoshi's Bitcoin was able to build this virtual cash system that in many ways was similar to peer-to-peer networks used for online file sharing.

As Bitcoin rose to prominence, other cryptocurrencies soon popped up. There are currently hundreds of different cryptocurrencies used globally, but among the market leaders, the cryptocurrency that is generating a lot of attention among financial institutions and industry experts is Ripple. Ripple was created by David Schwartz, Arthur Britto, and Ryan Fugger and released in 2012. As of January 2018, Ripple is now the third largest cryptocurrency based on market capitalization.

What has enabled Ripple to leapfrog to the top of the biggest cryptocurrencies of today? How is it different from Bitcoin and other virtual currencies being touted today? In the Chapter One, we will look at the history of Ripple and how it has evolved into something beyond just another virtual currency platform.

Chapter One: History Of Ripple

Ripple is a creation of Arthur Britto, Ryan Fugger, and David Schwartz. But long before the launch of Ripple in 2012, the beginnings of this platform were already developed by Fugger in 2004 through a payment protocol known as Ripplepay. Fugger is a web developer based in Vancouver, British Columbia, and he was intent on developing a local exchange trading platform for use within the Vancouver area. Inevitably, his idea was also to design a virtual monetary system with decentralized features and with its own currency being traded by users. The RipplePay system was launched in 2005 offering safe payment options to online community users within a global network.

In this sense, the concept of Ripple as a monetary system is actually older than Bitcoin, although Bitcoin became the largest and is still the leading cryptocurrency to date. Within the Ripple network, currency is represented as debt, and transactions are composed of balances moving on credit lines from the payer (or sender) to the receiver. Ripple's main foundation is an establishment of a reliable network or trust relationship, otherwise called a credit line, but between users instead of financial institutions. The decentralization concept was applied as all users within the Ripple network became banking institutions on their own, with the ability to issue, accept, and process transactions or loans.

With the launch of Fugger's Ripplepay, thousands of users signed up to become part of the communities. It was a successful project, although the communities themselves were often small and separate from each other. To become part of the network, one had to know someone who was already part of the network, and this kept Ripplepay more exclusive and slowed its growth and adoption. Also, the software being used was centralized, despite Fugger's intent to design a virtual monetary system with equal distribution. The system monitoring transactions, balances, and credit lines required a central database.

Another predecessor of the Ripple protocol as we know it today was the system designed by Jed McCaleb, along with Britto and Schwartz, who were all designers of the eDonkey network. By May of 2011, they were working on the design of a digital currency system which relied on transaction verification as approved by the members of the network, in sharp contrast to Bitcoin, which utilizes a mining process based on blockchain ledgers. What this new system was built to do was to remove the need for a centralized exchange altogether, thus speeding up the process. Aside from the original authors, E-Loan and Prosper founder Chris Larsen also joined the development team in August 2012. Larsen was intent on improving on the original ideas of the Ripple system and providing an advantage over Bitcoin.

Opencoin Is Born

The new Ripple system had the advantage, of course, of having seasoned and knowledgeable cryptocurrency experts already in its development stages. McCaleb, for instance, had founded the Bitcoin exchange platform MtGox, while another developer, Stefan Thomas, had developed BitcoinJS. Armed with their concept for a virtual currency, McCaleb and Larsen met with Fugger, who consulted with several long-time members of the Ripple network before agreeing to work with the team. The partnership led to the foundation of OpenCoin, which is Ripple's parent company.

Fugger's concepts remain very much visible in the Ripple system, as OpenCoin's payment protocol, dubbed as Ripple Transaction Protocol or RTXP, relied heavily on Fugger's original ideas. The protocol increased the speed of financial transactions between two parties, and the direct transfer eliminated the usual wait times and additional fees tacked on by traditional banking institutions. RTXP was also compatible with any state-backed currency, so trading was possible for US dollars, euros, yen, even gold and airline miles.

What the new protocol was able to accomplish, unlike its predecessors, was solving the problem of separate small communities within the Ripple network. With the use of the special and exclusive currency of XRP within the platform, Ripple moved away from the debt-based concept, so the virtual currency can be transferred between Ripple addresses. This linked up communities and allowed for greater exchange freedom, unlike in the previous iterations wherein you could only send money to those within your trust network. All a user had to do was convert the money to XRP, so it can be sent through the network, with all transactions being encoded into the ledger as well.

Gateways For Users

The new Ripple protocol was also able to solve the problem of user expansion through the use of gateways. A gateway acts as a conduit of credit or an entry point into the network. This opens up the use of Ripple to those who are interested in using the protocol but are not yet connected to anyone who is already in the network. A gateway is a commercial service provider acting as the first point of transaction between the user and the recipient, with the ability to also utilize various gateways at any given point of time, helping to maintain decentralization.

In order to keep the network secure, OpenCoin designed Ripple around a common ledger, also relying on a single network of servers that validate transactions and compare records to maintain accuracy. Banks, providers, or users could own servers, creating an independent validation network.

Investors Provide Funding

Soon, OpenCoin's protocol was attracting attention, and investors were expressing interest. Some of the earliest investors in OpenCoin included technology venture capitalists Andreessen Horowitz, Lightspeed Venture Partners, FF Angel IV, Bitcoin Opportunity Fund, and Vast Ventures. OpenCoin also soon received funding from Google Ventures and IDG Capital Partners. With the funding infused from high-profile investment groups, OpenCoin's Ripple protocol rose in prominence. By July of 2013, XRP Fund II, LLC was incorporated into a subsidiary of OpenCoin, and in the following days announced that it was launching Bitcoin Bridge.

The Bitcoin Bridge linked Bitcoin and Ripple protocols, effectively allowing users within the Ripple network to send money to Bitcoin addresses. It also allowed merchants to accept any type of currency, so users were able to keep their money in a currency apart from Bitcoin or XRP. With the Bitcoin Bridge, the need for a central exchange was eliminated.

Rebranding To Ripple Labs

OpenCoin officially rebranded to Ripple Labs Inc. on September 26, 2013. Chris Larsen stayed as the Chief Executive Officer of Ripple Labs. Also, Ripple was officially released as free software, with the Ripple reference server becoming open source under ISC license. With Ripple officially becoming open source software, the peer-to-peer protocol and its features and tools became available to the user community which then became responsible for maintaining the entire network.

One of the biggest criticisms of Ripple at the beginning was that it was still, in essence, centralized. Apart from its web client, the Ripple network was still under the control of OpenCoin/Ripple Labs prior to the open source announcement, with the company able to make modifications to the Ripple protocol with no need for consultation. With the source code opening, all users could not start their own gateway or full node, and Ripple will continue even if, for some reason, Ripple Labs ceased to exist. Validators within the Ripple system, however, are still recommended by Ripple Labs for security, such as universities, non-profit organizations, banks, corporations, and other institutions.

Integration With Banks

Ripple took a major step towards a greater presence in mainstream financial markets when it moved to greater and increasing integration with banks, starting with Fidor Bank of Germany in May 2014. Fidor Bank was the first major bank to offer Ripple as a payment option to existing customers. Within the same year, two other banks, Cross River Bank and CBW Bank, both based in the United States, announced partnerships with Ripple. Meanwhile, payment services provider Astropay also joined the Ripple network that year, opening the protocol as an option for users in the seven Latin American countries it was servicing.

Also considered a major partnership for Ripple was its integration with ZipZap. The money transfer service provider, a competitor of Western Union, was already one of the earliest partners of Ripple, offering customers the ability to send payments in the digital currency and as an alternative to other more expensive payment methods and services. As Ripple began to be integrated by more and more institutions, Western Union soon followed suit, opening its system to the virtual currency.

The focus of Ripple Labs has been the development of the protocol as an alternative financial service option for its users who want quick transactions and the elimination of banking fees. Financial institutions saw Ripple as a remittance option for customers, and a payment provider for retailers, corporations, and banks. As Ripple began to be integrated by large financial institutions and financial service providers, its price value rose dramatically, with market capitalization exceeding other cryptocurrencies that were already more established.

Among the biggest partnerships Ripple Labs was able to initiate was one with Earthport, a worldwide payment service which operated in more than 60 countries and included HSBC and Bank of America among its clients. Intrabank transfers using Ripple were soon being adopted by the Commonwealth Bank of Australia, with its CIO David Whiteing publicly stating that he believes digital currency such as Ripple is the future of consumer payments. Whiteing also mentioned that he sees Ripple and other non-asset based vendors as where the industry is headed, and he wants his bank to be part of the wave of the future particularly in payment transfers between CBA's subsidiaries.

Ripple's partnership with Germany's Fidor Bank is of particular interest. The German financial institution is a digital-only bank, with all services and transactions done online and with no physical branches. Fidor Bank was founded in 2009 and has been hailed as a trendsetter in offering banking services aimed at consumers who are increasingly doing their financial transactions online. Fidor Bank has also expanded into the United Kingdom and the United States, specifically targeting millennials via digital-only accounts. The digital bank partnered with Ripple Labs to offer a real-time international money transfer service, aside from its other forays with cryptocurrency exchanges.

Expansion Speeds Up

As large financial institutions cozied up to Ripple, it continued to expand its operations worldwide. Ripple Labs Asia Pacific, headquartered in Sydney, Australia, was opened in April of 2015 to cater to the rapid demand for Ripple's payment services in the Asia Pacific region. The office was also setup to more efficiently manage and oversee the transactions offered to Ripple Labs partners and users in the Asia Pacific markets, particularly those with existing relationships with European and American counterparts.

The expansion to the Asia Pacific region put Ripple in the center of a market that has seen dramatic growth in cross-border payments. In 2013 alone, cross-border payments in the region topped $200 billion, while intra-Asia trade reached $3 trillion the year before. It was forecast to overtake intra-Europe trade flows by 2016 and become the world leader. Ripple Labs Asia Pacific's office aggressively recruited a workforce of architects, integration engineers, and other professionals to oversee the expansion into Australia, New Zealand, China, Southeast Asia, Japan, and the Middle East.

Ripple's European presence, however, was not to be neglected, despite the attention to Asia Pacific. As European demand for Ripple's services also continued to grow, the company opened its London office in March of 2016. The expansion came as more European banks warmed to the idea of using Ripple's distributed ledger technology and offering Ripple's payment services to their customers. In particular, Ripple boasted a virtual currency and payment network that could potentially save European banks up to 60% of associated costs in global interbank payment settlements.

In June of the same year, Ripple opened another European office, this time in Luxembourg. Regarded as one of the centers of the European Union and being the headquarters of many agencies and institutions of the European Union, Luxembourg is also the top investment fund center in the continent, ranking second globally behind the United States. Luxembourg has also been aggressively attracting top finance and technology companies, making it a leading financial and banking capital.

Ripple's expansion to Luxembourg placed it at the apex of the global financial industry and opened its open protocol to more networks and international companies. With Luxembourg's reputation for neutrality and an openness to the latest financial technologies and modern banking solutions, Ripple's own innovations and creative drive found a perfect home.

Sure enough, by September of 2016, a major announcement by several big names in the banking sector gave a tremendous boost to Ripple's standing in the cryptocurrency industry. Dubbed as the Global Payments Steering Group, the network was formed by Bank of America, Royal Bank of Canada, and Santander, along with Standard Chartered, UniCredit, CIBC, and Westpac

Banking Corporation. The international network was formed to sustain a payments network utilizing Ripple's protocol and distributed ledger solutions. The network aims to rival the inter-bank messaging of SWIFT, currently the most widely-used for transfers.

The list of banks and companies utilizing Ripple has continued to grow by leaps and bounds. Aside from the aforementioned groups, other partnerships are ongoing with Accenture, UBS, American Express, Cambridge Global Payments, Star One Credit Union, Shanghai Huarui Bank, National Bank of Abu Dhabi, Davis + Henderson, BMO Financial Group, and more. Meanwhile, institutions that have launched system tests or experiments with Ripple include DBS Group Holdings, Bank of Yokohama, Australia and New Zealand Banking Group, Bank of England, The 77 Bank, Royal Bank of Scotland, and others.

In Japan, as of mid-2017, 61 Japanese banks were already members of the SBI Ripple Asia, a network of banks using Ripple's technology for their payment transactions and settlements. Launched in the fourth quarter of 2016, SBI Ripple Asia started with 42 member-banks, and to date has a network representing over 80% of Japan's banking assets.

Where does Ripple stand now? As of January 2018, Ripple is the third largest cryptocurrency based on market capitalization. With a market cap of $61 billion dollars, it is holding its own behind market leaders Bitcoin (market cap of $215 billion) and Ethereum (market cap of $109 billion). In terms of trade volume, Ripple is not far behind

Ethereum, with a 30-day average (as of this writing) at $119 billion, behind Ethereum's $144 billion. Bitcoin still leads in trade volume, with a 30-day average of $438 billion.

Presently, Ripple is also among the most relied on by banks and payment networks because of its superior technology, payment settlements and infrastructure. Also to Ripple's advantage is the active participation of many established names as its validators in its growing network, with institutions such as WorldLink, Swedish ISP, Microsoft, CGI, Bahnhof, and the Massachussetts Institute of Technology among the more than 50 validators.

With all these credentials, it looks like there is no way to go but up for Ripple as a virtual currency and as a provider of payment settlement technologies to global firms. In the next chapter, let us examine more closely how Ripple works, and what sets it apart from other cryptocurrency networks in the market. Why are traditional corporations and financial service providers embracing Ripple and realizing its potential for the future? A look at the design of Ripple will explain this more clearly.

Chapter Summary

- Ripple is the brainchild of Arthur Britto, David Schwartz, and Ryan Fugger.

- The main concepts of Ripple were set forth in 2004 by Fugger in his payment protocol, Ripplepay.
- The first iteration of Ripplepay was a moderate success, although communities became small and disparate.
- The software of Ripplepay was centralized, with a system for monitoring credit lines, balances, and transactions.
- The protocol for Ripple as we know it today came from Jed McCaleb of the eDonkey network, along with Britoo and Schwartz. They worked on a digital currency design relying on verification from members of the network.
- Several other key members of the early development of Ripple were Chris Larsen and Stefan Thomas, who all had prior experience with Bitcoin exchanges.
- OpenCoin merged the concepts along with Fugger's groundwork for Ripple, and the Ripple Transaction Protocol was launched. It increased the speed of payments and eliminated much of the additional fees.
- Early investors in OpenCoin included Vast Ventures, Bitcoin Opportunity Fund, Andreessen Horowitz, and Lightspeed Venture Partners. Google Ventures and IDG Capital Partners also provided funding.

- On September 26, 2013, OpenCoin changed its name to Ripple Labs Inc. and released the Ripple software as open source, opening it to the user community.
- Ripple's priority was integration with established banks and financial institutions, as it inked partnerships with Fidor Bank, ZipZap, Earthport, Commonwealth Bank of Australia, and other big names.
- By 2015-2016, Ripple was expanding to Asia Pacific and Europe, setting up offices in Sydney, London, and Luxembourg.
- Ripple's protocol was adopted by the Global Payments Steering Group, which counted Bank of America, Standard Chartered, CIBC, Westpac Banking Corporation, and Royal Bank of Canada among its constituents.
- In Japan, more than 60 banks currently are part of SBI Ripple Asia, which used Ripple's protocol for their payment settlements.

Today, Ripple is the third largest cryptocurrency based on market capitalization and trade volume.

Chapter Two: How Does Ripple Work?

Ripple refers to both the cryptocurrency XRP, as well as its digital payment protocol which is being used by various banks and institutions all over the world. To understand the world of Ripple and what sets it apart from the rest, you will first need to understand the basic workings of the system itself.

In reality, Ripple has become more known for its payment solution and technology than for its cryptocurrency. This is because within the Ripple system, money can be transferred in whatever form the users prefer. The system allows transactions in US dollar, Euro, Yen, Pound, Bitcoin, Ether, Litecoin, or XRP. This open source platform makes Ripple easy to integrate into various other existing infrastructure and protocols, which is an advantage for both Ripple and its community of users.

The Ripple system operates in a very close system of trust between different parties, and there is also a system of debt or credit lines involved in the process. To simplify the process, the sender will log on to his Ripple gateway (conduit or agent), deposits the money into this Ripple gateway, and sends the instruction for the funds to be released to the receiver. The receiver will receive the funds by logging on to his preferred receiver.

In this Ripple payment protocol, the transfers are not limited to money. Cryptocurrencies can be sent as long as the gateways are able to transact in them. Gold and other precious materials may also be transacted. The important thing is to find gateways that are willing and able to perform the transaction.

Suppose, for instance, that the sender wants to send $1000 to the receiver, but the sender's own gateway does not have a direct trust relationship with the receiver's gateway. What the Ripple algorithm will attempt to do is to find a chain, or several intermediary gateways which can act as the conduit for the transaction to go through. Ripple's protocol will try to find the shortest and quickest link between gateways in order to process the transaction.

Now, what if the Ripple network has attempted to find a chain of trust between two different gateways to process a transfer, but cannot locate a chain? This is where the Ripple cryptocurrency or XRP comes into play. XRP may be used within the Ripple network to convert money or goods being transferred. All currencies and goods will have an XRP price, and the sender can then choose to convert to XRP, send the XRP through the chain, to get to the receiver. The receiver, meanwhile, can opt to convert the XRP back to the original currency from his own gateway.

In the Ripple network, users are transacting currencies, commodities, and other units of value seamlessly. Chris Larsen, one of the co-founders of Ripple Labs and who also has extensive experience in digital finance (having founded e-Loan and Prosper), referred to the Ripple protocol as "HTTP for money". Larsen likens Ripple to gold as a standard of currency, because gold requires liquidity, trust, and utility to become a standard. "It's analogous to the Bitcoin networks. Any user can use the protocol just like they would HTTP. You can build on top of it without licensing it from anybody," according to Larsen.

Who or what can be a gateway in the world of Ripple? A gateway can be any user or organization allowing other users to either channel money into the Ripple network or take money from its liquidity pool. Because Ripple is open source and has a built-in decentralized exchange characteristic, gateways are visible to the public and can be trusted for the transactions of users.

The gateways can accept a currency deposit from a user and issue a balance into the distributed ledger, while also redeeming balances against deposits when any currency is withdrawn by a user. Gateways can be compared to banks in the traditional sense, but within the Ripple protocol, gateways only use one global ledger. Various gateways have their own policies in place regarding what data to require from users.

Some popular gateways in the Ripple network include Ripple Fox, Gatehub, Bitstamp, The Rock Trading, Mr. Ripple, and Tokyo JPY. A gateway serves as credit intermediary between two users, allowing the transaction to push through. Any person, company, or organization may register and start functioning as a gateway within the Ripple platform, and this authorizes the entity to become a middleman for payment transfers, liquidity, and currency exchange.

This digital network is where XRP is mostly used, foremost as a type of bridge currency between other fiat or cryptocurrencies. The gateways in the Ripple network will provide an XRP price of cash, cryptocurrency, or other currencies they are transacting. A user is able to convert anything to the corresponding XRPs, then proceed with the transfer using the gateway's trust chain, after which the receiver can receive and convert it back.

When XRP is sent within the Ripple platform, it has immediate settlement. The transaction is final, and ownership immediately changes. XRP transfers require less intermediaries or trust chains, so there are also less transaction fees. The process is also faster. The quick transaction time is one of the biggest advantages of Ripple over its counterparts in the traditional banking sector. Transfer payments can be settled within just a matter of seconds in the platform even if there are millions of transactions going on simultaneously. This is in sharp contrast to the standard number of days or even weeks it can take to process a wire transfer between two banks in different countries. Fees are also very minimal compared to the usual transaction fees for cross-border payments charged by banks.

Within the Ripple network, XRP is the only currency that does not require trust to be sent. Unlike in other currencies or commodities where users must establish trust with gateways, XRP can be sent through exchanges or conversions between the intended currency and XRP. So, if a user has no other way to process a transaction, XRP is the currency that can make it happen.

The Ripple platform utilizes what is known as a distributed ledger, or a common shared ledger. Often also termed a consensus ledger, this is a distributed database with the purpose of storing all the data regarding Ripple accounts and activities. Within the Ripple network, this ledger is maintained by a large network of validating servers, all working independently of each other, with constant updates and comparisons of their transaction records to ensure utmost accuracy.

Servers for validation may be owned and maintained by any person, organization, or bank. Validating servers currently include retailers, major banks, currency traders, and market-makers. When a transaction is being processed, the validating servers must agree that it is a valid transaction. Once consensus is reached, the transfer will be processed. The company itself, Ripple Labs, continues to develop the protocol, although the protocol is already open-source.

Many banks are being integrated into the Ripple network, with the assistance of Ripple Labs itself. When banks integrate Ripple's protocol into their cross-border payment systems, customers can send payments in their own currencies without necessarily having to use XRP, or any other cryptocurrency for that matter. The process is faster and cheaper than usual processing times and transaction fees required by banks. The integration with banks is a revenue source for Ripple Labs, aside from the large share of XRPs still held by the company.

Every few seconds, a new consensus ledger is created within Ripple. This ledger contains the most recent and accurate record of transactions that happened in the system. The peer-to-peer ledger contains information such as the settings for every account, the balance or trust lines between accounts, existing offers in the distributed exchange, various network settings like reserve amounts or transaction fees, a time stamp, and other critical data.

Client applications or users are constantly signing and sending transactions to the distributed servers, or also called nodes. Nodes accept and process the transactions, ensuring that the transfers are valid. Client applications being used to process transactions in the Ripple network include gateways, electronic trading platforms or exchanges, and mobile or web-based wallets. Nodes in Ripple may be described as either tracking nodes (mostly acting as transaction distributors or responding to ledger queries) or validating nodes (they also add information to the ledger aside from distributing transactions and processing queries).

Transactions may take time to distribute, as the nodes are not always working with the same candidate transactions simultaneously. When a transaction is accepted, it is called a candidate, and candidate transactions may be propagated throughout the Ripple network. To account for the delay, however, Ripple uses a consensus process to maintain consistency across all nodes in the Ripple ledger.

In the consensus process, the validating nodes will determine a section or subset of candidate transactions to be submitted for the next ledger (keeping in mind, of course, that ledgers are generated every few seconds). Consensus refers specifically to the process wherein nodes relay sets of candidate transactions, also known as proposals. As the nodes update these proposals and communicate with each other in the peer-to-peer network, an agreement is reached on these transactions.

An integral part of the consensus process is the chosen validators. The chosen validators act as a superior set of peers in the network, and they are relied on to maintain the integrity of nodes evaluating each proposal. This is a very important part of the trust-based relationship within the world of Ripple. Validators are selected with the strict confidence that they will not attempt any collusion or concerted effort to falsify the data being sent to the network and added to the ledger. Ripple validators currently include the Massachusetts Institute of Technology, WorldLink, AT Tokyo Corporation, Bahnhof, Microsoft, and CGI.

This is just an overview of the basic concept of Ripple. There are many facets to the overall operation and system of Ripple, but a basic understanding of how it works is essential to fully grasp how Ripple is shaking up financial transactions as we know them today. In the next chapter, we will compare Ripple to some of the other leading cryptocurrency platforms in use today, including Bitcoin, Litecoin, and Ethereum. What sets Ripple apart from its counterparts, and what are the advantages of Ripple?

Chapter Summary

- Ripple is both a type of digital currency, or cryptocurrency, and a digital payment protocol in open source format.

- Within the Ripple platform, fiat currency, virtual currency, and even goods and commodities may be transferred by users.
- The Ripple platform operates in a system of trust established between parties. Credit lines are involved in the process.
- Ripple uses gateways as agents between users attempting to process transactions.
- The Ripple algorithm will try to either establish a transaction between two gateways with pre-existing trust relationships, or find a chain or a path of intermediary gateways to allow the transfer to process.
- When a transfer cannot be processed using any existing trust chains, the currency can be converted to XRP, Ripple's in-house cryptocurrency. Both the sender and the receiver can opt to send or receive the transfer in XRP or another currency.
- All currencies and other goods being traded in Ripple have a corresponding XRP price.
- Ripple uses a distributed or common shared ledger where transactions are logged. A new ledger is generated every few seconds.
- Validation is performed by servers maintained by various entities checking to make sure the transactions are valid.
- Ripple also utilizes a consensus process where sets of transactions called proposals are updated and approved to the ledger.

Chosen validators are a set of peers in the Ripple network selected to ensure the accuracy of data.

Chapter Three: Ripple And Other Cryptocurrencies

As cryptocurrencies continue to grab the headlines and become the center of discussions in various media outlets, interested parties want to know what their differences are. After all, there must be fundamentally sound strategies that set apart the leading cryptocurrency platforms, and it would be essential to understand the reason behind the striking success of the biggest cryptocurrencies compared to other lesser known counterparts.

The cryptocurrency trend, by all measurements, is here to stay for at least the foreseeable future. Virtual currencies are being touted as the future in finances, and many cryptocurrency platforms have moved on from just providing an alternative digital currency to even taking over much of the processes and functionalities of traditional banks and financial service providers. The initial pushback of the banking and finance industry against cryptocurrencies has largely been replaced by a growing acceptance of its potential as the currency of the next generation.

Bitcoin And Ripple

Bitcoin is by far the leading cryptocurrency in the market today, and is still arguably the benchmark or standard by which other cryptocurrencies, including Ripple, are measured. Because of this distinction, comparisons between Ripple and Bitcoin are often at the top of minds of potential investors and information seekers, what with Bitcoin's ubiquitous market presence and incessant media attention.

Since its inception, Bitcoin truly was envisioned to be what it continues to do best today - a peer-to-peer virtual currency protocol. Bitcoin is the brainchild of Satoshi Nakamoto, who is either one person or a group of people concealing their identity under one name, depending on who you ask. This cryptocurrency was the first successful decentralized digital currency in the world, operating without one administrator or any backing from a central bank or governing authority.

While Bitcoin has continued to evolve, it has remained largely a cryptocurrency protocol, staying true to its original purpose. In fact, Bitcoin has become so successful in this area that it now exceeds the value of any fiat or state-backed currencies. For a brief period, it was also valued higher than gold. To this day, Bitcoin is still regarded as the mother of all cryptocurrencies.

In this regard, Ripple is fundamentally different from Bitcoin because, at the onset, Ripple's original design was to serve as a global payment system and alternative remittance network, while also providing a fast and secure currency exchange platform. Over time, as Ripple's infrastructure has grown, its network has also given birth to its own cryptocurrency, the XRP. This comparison is evident in the expansion plans and focus that Bitcoin and Ripple have become involved in over the years. While Bitcoin has grown by leaps and bounds as a virtual currency, Ripple has become more known for its payment protocol.

If you use Ripple, for instance, one of the virtual currencies you can trade in is Bitcoin, and because of the widespread acceptance and trade volume of Bitcoin, you will be sure to find almost no difficulty in trading Bitcoin within the Ripple network, or most other cryptocurrency platforms for that matter. The main strength of Ripple, on the other hand, has been to pave the way for global financial transactions to be processed securely and quickly at almost no expense, regardless of the size of the trade.

Although Bitcoin as a cryptocurrency was the first decentralized virtual currency, the Ripple project itself preceded Bitcoin. Ripple's roots date back to Ryan Fugger's initial concepts in the mid-2000s, although the XRP currency was not officially launched until 2013, or four years after Bitcoin had already hit the market.

One of the main differences between Bitcoin and Ripple is the mining process of their currencies. Bitcoins are created by users of the currency through a process that is called mining, which refers to a record-keeping service performed via computer processing power. Bitcoin miners are constantly mining and earning Bitcoins. The maximum number of Bitcoins that can be mined is 21 million. Of these Bitcoins, 980,000 belong to Satoshi Nakamoto.

On the other hand, the creators of Ripple have already created 100 billion Ripples to be used within the networks. 55 billion Ripples will be made available to users, partners, and charitable groups. Ripple Labs holds about 62 percent of the supply of XRPs.

The ownership hierarchies and governance policies between Bitcoin and Ripple are also readily apparent. Bitcoin is fully decentralized and open source, with ownership resting on its community. Because of the decentralized nature of Bitcoin, any upgrades or proposed changes to the system can be quite difficult to implement. In case developers want to introduce upgrades or changes to the network, they may utilize what is known as "soft forks" or backwards-compatible updates specifically for nodes to apply and reverse without disrupting the entire network.

Ripple, meanwhile, is also open source software, but it is owned by the private company Ripple Labs, which also can access the platform's internal ledger and implement changes or upgrades without consulting users. Developers need to get approval or consensus under the amendment system in place within Ripple. If a proposed amendment garners 80 percent support for at least two weeks, it will be applied to the entire system and newly-generated ledgers will then support the update.

Apart from the difference in decentralized governance between Bitcoin and Ripple, the way users can buy or sell the cryptocurrencies also can be compared. For Bitcoin buying, selling, or trading, users need to use the centralized exchange within the platform. For buying, selling, or trading XRPs, meanwhile, the currency can be procured or sold within the secure network itself, allowing for more liquidity.

The speed of transactions varies greatly between Bitcoin and Ripple as well. The average transaction time for Bitcoin is about ten minutes. Recently, Bitcoin users have been given the option to pay a miner to prioritize or speed up their transaction time, for an additional fee of around $30. With this arrangement, a transaction in Bitcoin can be reduced to half.

Ripple dramatically cuts this transaction time down to 4 seconds. The difference lies in Ripple's off-ledger transaction feature, wherein a node will process a group of transactions first before adding them to the ledger. This way, multiple transactions are being processed without having to sacrifice security or accuracy. Ripple has a minimum transaction cost which is in place to avoid too much congestion or overloading in the system. Transaction fees are very low for Ripple, at a fraction of a cent on average.

As far as the data stored in their networks, there are also fundamental differences between Bitcoin and Ripple. Ripple tracks various information and is able to store data about account balance, creditworthiness, and other essential details. In the Bitcoin network, however, only Bitcoin movement or transaction paths are tracked. In fact, Bitcoin uses addresses linked to owners, so although transactions are publicly visible on the blockchain, the owners of the Bitcoin addresses are not revealed. Users may even generate a new Bitcoin address for every transaction on the network.

As far as the general direction and future goals of their platforms, Bitcoin and Ripple are heading towards different directions. Bitcoin is more intent on maintaining its decentralized approach to virtual currency and maintaining its lead as a secure digital currency used all over the world. Ripple's focus, on the other hand, has been on promoting its platform as well as its cryptocurrency to traditional financial clients, emphasizing the speed of its network and efficiency in transferring assets.

Ethereum And Ripple

Another cryptocurrency that has risen to the top of the list is Ethereum. It is the second largest cryptocurrency to date based on market capitalization. Ethereum is the name of the blockchain company that created the digital currency Ether, but these days Ethereum is now used to refer to either the currency or the company behind it.

Ethereum uses blockchain technology, very similar to Bitcoin, but its protocol and requirements are different because of the use of smart contracts. A smart contract is an agreement encoded digitally into a blockchain, and once both parties in the contract have fulfilled the necessary requirements, the deal or agreement is then executed.

This system of smart contracts is vastly different to Ripple's trust-based and credit-based structure. However, both Ethereum and Ripple have emerged as the leading solutions providers for businesses and organizations wanting to streamline and increase the efficiency of their transactions and arrangements. While Ripple is mostly used for payment settlements and transfers, Ethereum has been expanding into an ecosystem for developers and investors looking for improved functions and applications utilizing a blockchain and a programming language.

Central to this Ethereum platform is the Ethereum Virtual Machine, or EVM, which allows users to encode smart contracts and applications, while also acting as a currency exchange. Users who want to be able to access the EVM and its treasure trove of applications and smart contracts must use the Ether currency, and Ether may also be used to pay for various fees or services within Ethereum. Of course, it is also a digital currency.

You can think of Ethereum as more of a community of entrepreneurs, investors, and developers who are looking for smarter ways to enforce contracts and business arrangements. With more and more developers using EVM, the community is growing, and its currency is also going up in value. Meanwhile, because the community is expanding, Ethereum is becoming more and more self-contained and self-sufficient because of the decentralized applications being converted to its platform.

Far from developing its own ecosystem, on the other hand, Ripple is integrating with banks, companies, organizations, and financial service providers, allowing its protocol to be experimented with and applied by strategic partners. As such, Ripple is gaining a foothold in the banking and financial industry's transactions. In this perspective, the Ripple currency becomes less of a priority, as Ripple Labs seeks instead to focus on a long-term and sustainable future as the preferred payment settlement technology worldwide.

It is interesting to note that, for both Ripple and Ethereum, the virtual currency is more of a by-product or a result of the innovative characteristics of their respective platforms. Ripple's XRP is a go-to currency for transactions within Ripple, but all other fiat and digital currencies are accepted and traded. Ether, on the other hand, is what is needed to fund the smart contracts and decentralized applications within Ethereum. Beyond their respective spheres of influence, Ripple and Ethereum are still forming their identities as cryptocurrencies, but their originating platforms are already integrated in modern business technology.

Litecoin And Ripple

Litecoin is another digital currency that has attracted its own share of attention. This peer-to-peer cryptocurrency does share many similarities to Bitcoin, including its open source protocol, cryptography-based infrastructure, and decentralized nature. Litecoin was created by former Google employee Charlie Lee. From its release on October of 2011, Litecoin has also experienced a surge in growth, becoming one of the top five cryptocurrencies.

While Ripple still leads Litecoin in terms of market capitalization, Litecoin has been increasing in trading volume. Many investors are attracted to Litecoin as an alternative cryptocurrency because it has faster transaction confirmation compared to Bitcoin, at an average of 2.5 minutes. Compared to Ripple, of course, this is still an advantage held by the XRP network.

For some period of time after its release, Litecoin was the second largest cryptocurrency in the market, coming in just behind Bitcoin. Because of its similarities to Bitcoin, Litecoin was considered as the next alternative especially as

Bitcoin prices surged and investors looked for the next virtual currency that would trend upward. However, Litecoin was soon surpassed by other cryptocurrencies offering more than just the digital currency alternative. Ethereum, for instance, with its evolving ecosystem of smart contracts and decentralized applications, soon overtook Litecoin in the second spot as more developers and merchants flocked to its platform.

Meanwhile, Ripple's advantage has been its adoption by established names in the financial sector and the perception that on top of its digital currency potential, the technology Ripple offers is here for the long-term and may even become the new standard in intra-bank and cross-border payment transactions. Litecoin's main selling point has been the faster transaction times and cheaper transaction costs compared to Bitcoin, but it remains to be seen whether this virtual currency platform can offer more attractive features than just being an alternative.

It has become apparent, then, that for cryptocurrencies to succeed in giving Bitcoin a run for its money, they must offer features and functionalities that entice investors, corporate entities, organizations, banking institutions, government agencies, enterprise users, and even personal users to switch to their platforms for more than just digital cash transfers. Ripple is more known for the services it offers although its XRP has also risen in public awareness.

Bitcoin Leads, Other Currencies Follow

As far as cryptocurrency values, the reality is that where Bitcoin goes, Ripple and the rest of the cryptocurrencies will follow, for the most part. In this era of virtual currencies, what has been the trend is a surge in the prices of Ripple, Ethereum, Litecoin, and other digital currencies such as Monero and Dash whenever Bitcoin's price is also going up. Investors see an upward trend in the value of Bitcoin as a positive sign for the rest of the cryptocurrencies, so investment also pours in for the rest of the segment.

On the other hand, when Bitcoin takes a hit, so do the other cryptocurrencies. In recent weeks, for instance, the price of one Bitcoin has fallen from its peak of around $20,000 at the end of 2017 to about $11,200 as of this writing. The rest of the cryptocurrencies have also seen this trend, reflecting the same downward trend as Bitcoin's before rebounding. According to market analysts, the overall cryptocurrency market may be normalizing and becoming more resilient to price volatilities that have been quite frequent in past quarters.

This puts Ripple right at the center of a potentially lucrative and financially rewarding apex of rising virtual coins. With its lower price, Ripple is still an investor-friendly gamble. In the next chapter, let us look at some ways you can invest, trade, or start getting your slice of the earnings in Ripple.

Chapter Summary

- As the leading cryptocurrency, Bitcoin is still the benchmark for other virtual currencies, including Ripple.
- Bitcoin has been designed as a peer-to-peer virtual currency from the start, while Ripple was created as a payment protocol, with the digital currency a by-product to facilitate transfers.
- Bitcoins are mined using computer processors, while XRPs were already created by Ripple Labs for distribution.
- Bitcoin is fully decentralized with no governing authority, while Ripple is owned by Ripple Labs. Both are open source software.
- Ripple has the definitive advantage over Bitcoin when it comes to transaction times, as it can process transactions in as little as 4 seconds, compared to the average 10 minutes for Bitcoin.
- The amount of information that can be stored in Ripple is also more extensive, compared to just transaction movements monitored in Bitcoin.
- Bitcoin is maintaining its trajectory as a virtual currency, while Ripple has focused more on promoting its platform for integration with other entities.

- The second leading cryptocurrency, Ethereum, is envisioned to be a self-supporting ecosystem of decentralized applications.
- Ethereum's main difference from other cryptocurrencies is its smart contracts enabling payments between entities.
- Ethereum operates on a contract-based system, while Ripple is more trust-based in structure.
- Both Ripple and Ethereum are thriving because of their solutions technologies geared towards businesses and organizational streamlining.
- Litecoin, another leading cryptocurrency, is a Bitcoin alternative offering faster transaction times and lower costs.

Positive trends in Bitcoin have benefitted Ripple and the other cryptocurrencies. Similarly, any downturns in the value of Bitcoin have usually spilled over to the other virtual currencies as well.

Chapter Four: Investing In Ripple

So, you are interested in investing in Ripple. How do you go about doing it? Remember that Ripple is more than just a virtual currency, and its potential to shake up how financial providers and banking institutions offer their services is interesting to watch. But as a consumer, you would want to start by investing first in the digital currency itself and becoming familiar with the world of Ripple.

One of the things going for you as a potential Ripple investor is the price of XRP. Right now, XRP is priced at around $2.25 per coin. This is very affordable compared to Bitcoin (currently priced at $11,513), Ether ($1,043), or Litecoin ($190). If you have limited capital at the moment or want to start smaller with less risk, just to see how things go and if cryptocurrency is something you would like to invest in, Ripple is a fairly manageable risk.

However, what is different with Ripple is it can be a little harder to procure than the other popular cryptocurrencies.

There are widely used applications like Coinbase where users can easily purchase other virtual coins, but Ripple is not readily available through these applications. Instead, what you will need to do first is to set up an account with a Ripple exchange.

There are several recommended exchanges for Ripple purchase. If you are using a credit or debit card and would like to purchase in US dollars or euros, Bitstamp is one of the more popular exchanges. You will need to open a Bitstamp account, and go through the account verification procedure. Once your account has been verified successfully, you can deposit funds into your Bitstamp account, then use these funds to purchase XRP at prevailing market rates. Bitstamp is based in Luxembourg, and aside from XRP, it also processes trading in Bitcoin, Litecoin, and Ethereum.

Another exchange recommended by Ripple is Kraken. The company is based in San Francisco, California, and is a leading exchange for investors wanting to buy cryptocurrencies using euros. You may also use US dollars and other currencies for both buying and selling virtual coins in Kraken.

Other popular XRP exchanges you can check out are Binance and Bitsane. These exchanges have similar requirements as far as setting up an account and going through verification procedures. Typically, when you go to their home page, you will see the current exchange prices for trading between different cryptocurrencies. As already mentioned, you will need to convert your fiat currency such as USD or euro into Bitcoin or Ether before you can purchase XRPs, so you will need to be aware how much the other cryptocurrencies are trading.

Once you already have an account setup with a cryptocurrency exchange, you can then use an application such as Coinbase to purchase Bitcoin, Ether, or another preferred virtual coin. This is convenient if you already have investments in other cryptocurrencies anyway. Once you have your Bitcoin or Ether, you can move it to your Ripple-recommended exchange and use it to purchase XRP. It may sound like a complicated process, but once you get the hang of it, this system of buying XRP is the most convenient way to purchase XRPs for the meantime, or at least until Ripples can be purchased directly from popular applications.

If you live in Europe, you may use a cryptocurrency brokerage service such as BitPanda. BitPanda is based in Austria and allows users to purchase XRPs using their credit card, but it is only available in European countries. For residents of the US or most other countries, the most convenient way is still to go through an exchange and set up an account, then purchase Bitcoin or Ether before transferring to the exchange for XRP purchase.

Ripple Wallets For Storage

Once you have purchased XRPs, it is recommended that you move it out of the exchange and store it elsewhere for security. This is advised for all cryptocurrencies. Users should remember not to store their virtual currencies within the exchange, because in case the exchange is hacked or is attacked virtually, there is a risk of losing your virtual money. Instead, what you should consider for storing your XRP is a Ripple wallet.

There are different types of wallets you may use for storing your Ripples. You can opt for a hardware wallet such as the Ledger Nano S. The Ledger Nano S supports XRP storage, and it is manufactured by Ledger, a Bitcoin security firm which has produced hardware wallets for various cryptocurrencies since 2014. Ledger is based in France.

The Nano S hardware wallet is easy to use and is recommended if you plan on storing your XRP for a longer period, meaning you do not plan on trading or selling any time soon. The Nano S is offline storage which makes it more secure than keeping your XRP on an online computer which is more vulnerable to hackers or attacks. Offline storage using Nano S is safer.

If you like to access your XRP through your Android or iOS smartphone, you may also opt for an Android or iOS wallet. Ripple wallets for Android or iOS let you access your account online, and send or receive XRPs, making it convenient for constant transfers or trading. For both iOS and Android, Toast Wallet is a popular open source Ripple wallet. Toast Wallet is also available as a desktop Ripple wallet, with versions for Windows, Mac and Linux. Storing your XRP on an Android, iOS, or desktop wallet is not as safe as keeping it on a hardware wallet, especially for long-term. If you will only need to store it for a few days, it should be fine (just take the necessary precautions in securing your device against malware).

At the moment, Ripple is still far from being widely accepted for purchases and other services, compared to Bitcoin and other cryptocurrencies already accepted by many online merchants or retailers. What you would want to do, in the meantime, is hold on to your XRP and monitor the price movements, making sure to look at price fluctuations and identify opportunities for either purchasing XRP at lower prices, or selling at higher prices. XRP as a digital currency is still in its early growth stage, although it has already shown remarkable progress and, indeed, is at the top of the sector because of the robust adoption by established financial names.

Ripple Focuses On Integration

Ripple is in a unique position as a cryptocurrency investment because while other digital currencies are being alternatives to fiat currencies and financial services provided by banks, Ripple's come-on is its integration and interconnection with the very payment providers and banks most customers still use regularly. In fact, Ripple markets itself as 'the world's only enterprise blockchain solution for global payments'.

As an interested investor in Ripple, you should note that as other virtual currencies are being strategized as asset class, Ripple is happy to extend itself as a tool or system for established banking systems globally. This contrasts with the goal of Bitcoin and most other digital currencies, which is to move the power of finance away from the big players. As such, Ripple has often been criticized as a cryptocurrency designed for the establishment; but, the innovations Ripple is bringing to the global financial sector benefits not just the head honchos of banks and investment firms, but also individual users sending payments and transferring money and other services worldwide.

Perception Of Stability And Long-Term Sustainability

Another advantage going for Ripple, from an investment point of view, is the long-term stability and lower volatility. The perception is that Ripple is a safer investment as a whole, mainly because it is not just relying on a cryptocurrency that is dramatically increasing in price, but also strengthening its foundation in other ventures and partnerships. This was proven when major financial institutions started adopting Ripple's payment protocols and integrating their systems to Ripple's technology. Integrations are big decisions for big banks, with potentially far-reaching effects, so unless these institutions see any technology as one that has a long-term viability, they will not be likely to capitulate to it regardless of demand.

This also gives Ripple somewhat of a fall back especially as cryptocurrencies have experienced some turbulent times. Because it has much more to offer than just a virtual currency, it seems poised to withstand any major upheavals in the cryptocurrency market should there be a major downturn. As seen in recent weeks, cryptocurrencies have taken a beating as far as market prices, although many analysts believe this is just the market correcting itself and stabilizing the prices of cryptocurrencies. Still, it would help to know that Ripple is not dependent only on a virtual currency that competes with Bitcoin. Rather, the backbone of the XRP currency is the payment protocol now being utilized as a long-term technology by big-name financial players, so Ripple is here to stay for the long-term even if turbulence hits the virtual currency side.

Not Competing With Other Virtual Currencies

In as far as its relationship with other cryptocurrencies, particularly Bitcoin, another good thing going for Ripple is it does not attempt to directly compete with Bitcoin as a virtual currency. Rather, Ripple is constantly looking to integrate not only with existing banking entities but also with Bitcoin and other cryptocurrencies. Presently, the Ripple platform supports transfers in fiat and crypto currencies, so users are not pressured to have to use XRP or convert to XRP before being able to process transfers.

Ripple understands that Bitcoin has established itself already as the mother of cryptocurrencies, so rather than trying to compete directly against it, it is looking for ways to exist side-by-side with the virtual currency behemoth. Besides, Ripple also realizes that as far as digital currencies are concerned, Bitcoin is the bellwether, by which the others rise and fall, and complementing Bitcoin would eventually work to XRP's favor.

What about some disadvantages or areas of concern regarding investing in Ripple? In the next chapter, let us go through some arguments or perceived weaknesses around Ripple as a potential investment.

Chapter Summary

- Ripple is a great entry-level cryptocurrency for investment because of its lower cost.
- At present, Ripple is not directly available for purchase through popular applications like Coinbase. It must be procured through a cryptocurrency exchange or brokerage service, converted from other virtual currencies like Ether or Bitcoin.
- Recommended exchanges for XRP include Bitstamp, Kraken, Bitsane, and Binance.
- Users are advised to refrain from storing XRPs in exchanges long-term. Hardware or software wallets are more advisable.

- A hardware wallet is offline storage and is more secure because it is not prone to hackers or online attacks.
- Instead of trying to migrate users from traditional financial services, Ripple is integration with existing infrastructure.
- Many investors see Ripple as a good long-term investment with less volatility.
- With increased focus on its payment solutions for global transactions, Ripple has longevity and adaptability.

Ripple is also working with, rather than competing head on, with other cryptocurrencies, especially Bitcoin.

Chapter Five: Areas Of Concern For Ripple

Any good investor with sound decision-making skills would look at both the positive and negative side of a potential investment. This is necessary in order to calculate risk and mitigate the effects, as well as to make an informed decision that would yield long-term benefits. In the consideration of cryptocurrencies such as Ripple, you should also look at the areas of concern, aside from the benefits.

Centralized Nature

Perhaps the biggest area of concern regarding Ripple is the issue of centralization. Unlike Bitcoin which is decentralized to its core, Ripple is still privately-owned and subject to the immediate control of Ripple Labs, despite the moves towards open-source protocol. The platform itself is still very much centralized, although this is still a work in progress and may somehow change in the near future. Still, the lack of decentralization in the Ripple network is enough for many cryptocurrency watchers to steer clear.

XRP Distribution

In relation to the decentralization issue, many critics of Ripple also bring up the realities regarding the distribution of XRPs, of which Ripple Labs still controls most of the tokens. As already mentioned in previous chapters, Ripple Labs already created 100 billion XRPs and set aside a portion of it for distribution in the network. Ripple Labs, however, controls about 60% of the tokens, which is different from the situation with other cryptocurrencies, where creators or developers of the platform usually only keep a smaller fraction of the tokens, while opening the rest for selling or trading.

Ripple has been taking steps to increase the promotion and distribution of the XRP market, and the company put most of its controlled XRPs into escrow, effectively unlocking up to 1 billion XRPs every month for the next few years. This has helped to ease concerns that, with most of the tokens controlled by the company, there may be a possibility of cashing out in the future and crashing the network altogether. Still, it has not helped much with the perception that Ripple could be thinking of ways to benefit tremendously from this as it controls the vast majority of the XRPs.

This issue became a bigger discussion as Ripple's relationship with its founders has come into question. One of the founders of Ripple, Jed McCaleb, turned heads in 2014 when he made the announcement that he was selling his 9 billion XRPs which he was awarded because of his role in starting the company. While this would have freed up more distribution of XRPs into the system, McCaleb's announcement had an opposite effect as it caused a big decline in the value of XRP. For many, it signalled a loss of confidence in the very platform he helped to start.

The rest of the Ripple co-founders reached out to McCaleb to come to a settlement, after which an agreement was announced that the sale of those XRP units would be incremental over several years rather than all at once. The agreement is similar to an agreement with another Ripple co-founder, Arthur Britto. The root of the issue was the long-standing disagreements between McCaleb and Ripple CEO Chris Larsen regarding where to take Ripple's future, and differences of opinion regarding XRP distribution itself.

Too Close To Banking Industry?

There are also issues because of the close relationship Ripple has cultivated with banks and financial institutions globally. At the very core of the cryptocurrency trend, of course, is the goal of moving away from the oversight of state-backed central banks and governing authorities which control fiat currencies and also have a hand in dictating transaction costs. This move away from the big banks has fuelled much of the demand for cryptocurrencies, especially as cryptocurrencies have shown a remarkable resilience and ability to bounce back from volatility and losses.

Ripple, however, not only partners actively with major financial institutions, but also has ongoing integrations with banking systems upgrading their payment technologies. This has given XRP the dubious distinction of being a cryptocurrency for bankers, and raised many questions about possible privacy concerns or breaches in user data made available to the big banks, many of which the average cryptocurrency users are trying to avoid as much as possible.

The close relationship Ripple has with banks is a double-edged sword for the cryptocurrency platform. While it has enabled Ripple to gain the trust and cooperation of many financial giants including American Express, Canadian Imperial Bank of Commerce, National Australia Bank, Westpac Banking Corporation, Standard Chartered, Royal Bank of Canada and others, it has also caused Ripple to be avoided by those who are not keen on this partnership. Also, many who are drawn to cryptocurrency in the first place are buoyed by a desire to either revolutionize how the financial system works today, or simply to detach from it as much as they can.

Increased Competition From Permissioned Blockchains

Some analysts also believe that as Ripple Labs continues to bolster its partnership network, its XRP currency may eventually become either obsolete or shrink in value as the very protocol of Ripple brings about permissioned blockchains. How? Ripple's system of gateways, trust lines, and issuance give banks and financial entities the freedom to build their networks, transfer their assets on the network, and save on transaction fees.

Permissioned blockchains refer to networks that require an invitation from an existing member-organization before a new entity is given entry. As it turns out, permissioned blockchains are now the competition of Ripple because they are offering services for payments and cross-border transactions very similar to those offered by Ripple. Some permissioned blockchains are Hyperledger, Ethereum Enterprise Alliance, and R3 Corda. The only advantage Ripple has over these permissioned blockchains is XRP, as these networks do not have their own digital currencies.

What the competitors are now offering are different methods for securing the network and easing transactions instead of creating native assets or cryptocurrencies. In a lot of ways, these networks are succeeding in offering services as payment networks comparable to Ripple without having to manage a cryptocurrency. Over time, some analysts see this as potentially a cause for XRP to become obsolete, even though Ripple can weather the competition and remain the superior payment network solution for banks.

What does this mean for you as an investor? If competition between these payment networks continues to heat up, Ripple Labs may have to respond accordingly to stay relevant, and XRP may be seen as an unnecessary factor that can be disregarded. After all, if the future of payment networks becomes so multi-faceted that native assets are no longer needed, it will make no sense for Ripple to continue forcing the use of XRP. This could lead to a significant devaluation of XRP or its free distribution among current users, especially if it becomes apparent that XRP has become an unnecessary cost.

Security Risk

Experts also bring up a significant weakness in the security protocol of Ripple which is based largely on a 'small world' philosophy, or the notion that very person in the world is somehow connected to each other six steps away. In this thinking, two complete strangers are no more than six intermediary people away from each other, and this relationship can be used to gain trust and form a chain, thus allowing a transaction to process. While this open philosophy has led to a unique system and attracted the attention of the financial world, there are vulnerabilities as well.

A group of researchers from Purdue University, for instance, have called attention to the open and liquid structure of Ripple which may leave some nodes within the network vulnerable to attacks from outside, and cut off the users' access to their funds or wallets. As this security weakness has been identified, developers of Ripple should be able to identify the flaws and make the necessary corrections.

These are some pressing concerns to be aware of regarding Ripple. The state of the cryptocurrency itself is still very fluid, as is the general cryptocurrency market overall. Changes are happening daily, with demand increasing, prices updating, and new innovations or iterations being announced. Information you may see now, may become outdated in the next few days and weeks because of the evolving nature of Ripple and other cryptocurrencies. In the next chapter, let us look at where Ripple is currently, and why this virtual currency remains a viable investment opportunity for you to consider.

Chapter Summary

- The issue of decentralization remains one of the major concerns for Ripple, as Ripple Labs continues to own this platform.
- There are also concerns about the distribution of XRPs, although Ripple Labs has taken steps to correct the problem.

- Many have a negative perception regarding Ripple's ongoing relationships with many top banking institutions, which is contrary to how most other cryptocurrencies are moving away from the control of big banks as much as they can.
- Concerns have also been raised that as permissioned blockchains such as R3 Corda, Hyperledger, and Ethereum Enterprise Alliance step up the competition and offer similar features to Ripple's payment system, the native asset that is XRP may eventually become devalued or obsolete.

Attention has also been directed towards possible security flaws in certain nodes that are vulnerable to attacks, rendering access impossible for some users.

Chapter Six: Current Happenings In Ripple

Where is Ripple at the moment? Many changes and continuing innovations are being announced by Ripple, and these announcements give you an insight into where Ripple is channelling its efforts to further improve the platform.

More Deals And Partnerships

One major partnership announced at the start of 2018 is Ripple's deal with MoneyGram. This financial services provider, based in Dallas, Texas, offers money transfers, money orders, bill payment services, and other financial products to its customers in 200 countries worldwide. MoneyGram operates approximately 347,000 office locations globally, and is the second largest money transfer provider today.

As of January 2018, MoneyGram will start utilizing XRP in their payment systems, in an effort to make international payments faster, safer, and more cost-efficient for their customers. Funds will be available in real time, a significant improvement from the transaction times it currently takes for MoneyGram transfers to process now. In the deal, MoneyGram will be utilizing XRP via xRapid, Ripple's own liquidity product, to offer real-time foreign exchange settlements, lower the costs of FX, and provide instant feedback.

Alex Holmes, the CEO of MoneyGram, was optimistic about the partnership, saying, "Ripple is at the forefront of blockchain technology and we look forward to piloting xRapid. We're hopeful it will increase efficiency and improve services to MoneyGram's customers."

With this development, Ripple effectively provides a solution for yet another financial institution to rapidly transact money regardless of geographic location, as XRP provides for payment settlement in as little as three seconds. Wait times are dramatically reduced at a fraction of the cost.

Added Exchange Listings

In the last quarter of 2017, Ripple has also proven its mettle as among the fastest-rising stars of the cryptocurrency market in its inclusion into 50 global cryptocurrency exchanges. Because XRP is not available for direct purchase from applications like Coinbase, investors must course their procurement via exchanges. Ripple has gone from being listed on six different exchanges at the start of 2017 to over 50 global listings internationally, reflecting the growing demand for XRP and its perception as a reliable and scalable digital asset.

Exchanges that currently list XRP now include Bitstamp, Kraken, Bitso, Coinone, Korbit, Coincheck, Qryptos, Bitbank, Bitsane, BTC Markets, LiteBit, GateHub, and new additions GMOCoin (the top digital exchange in Japan), Huobi.pro (Singapore-based exchange averaging $787 million in daily trade volume), and CEX.IO (a leading exchange in the United Kingdom averaging $94 million in daily trade volume). The increase in the number of exchange listings for Ripple extends its accessibility and reach to more customers around the world and enables transfers to move faster and more efficiently.

American Express joins RippleNet

In 2017, Ripple also welcomed American Express to its growing blockchain network, specifically RippleNet which also boasts Cuallix, Credit Agricole and other major financial service providers among its members. The deal with American Express will enable the credit card giant to offer real-time business-to-business international payments to its customers, with plans for consumer transactions also in the works.

RippleNet has become the leading enterprise blockchain network, counting over 100 major financial entities and payment service providers from all over the world in its alliance. Aside from the aforementioned members, RippleNet also got TransferGo, IFX, Currencies Direct, Bexs Banco, Siam Commercial, SEB SBI Remit, AirWallex and others to get on board.

Cryptocurrency experts are mostly optimistic about the future of Ripple even as the virtual currency competition heats up. Ripple has been forecast to soon give Bitcoin a run for its money at the top of the cryptocurrency market capitalization. Glenn Hutchins, former chief of NASDAQ and among the first to recognize cryptocurrencies as essential financial investments, recently was asked what he thought about the future of cryptocurrency, to which he replied that those digital currencies offering more than just a currency, but an actual solution to a problem, will survive long-term.

"The price is a distraction - rather you should focus on the means of exchange. It's a very small nascent property that has potential to be transformative," according to Hutchins. "Bitcoin could be the wrong solution - and other tokens like Ethereum or Ripple could end up being the right answer ... Can you take that technology and use it as a solution for an important customer problem? That's the question investors need to monitor."

What was the problem that Ripple has identified and provided a solution for? To be very specific, it is the SWIFT system currently in place in the banking industry. SWIFT is short for the Society for Worldwide Interbank

Financial Telecommunication, which is a network allowing banks and financial institutions worldwide to send and receive information safely. Most international banks use SWIFT for sending payment orders. The problem with SWIFT is the transaction processing time, which can take a few days or weeks to verify.

Ripple offered a much faster and cheaper solution, and real-time transactions became a reality for even intra-bank and inter-bank transfers. Aside from the speed and lower cost, Ripple also capitalized on the growing acceptance of blockchain technology which is more secure and can hold off attacks or hackers. Speed, cost, and security are main concerns for the market that Ripple identified and targeted, and this has resulted into the robust growth Ripple is still experiencing.

This is not to say, of course, that Ripple is immune to upheavals or shocks that cryptocurrencies are still going through, especially at the beginning of 2018. Bitcoin, Ethereum, Ripple, Litecoin, and other digital currencies have seen their prices spiral downward in recent weeks as concerns over growing attempts to regulate their circulation in various markets around the world have worried investors.

In past instances, where Bitcoin experienced a sell-off, the funds that left were invested in other digital currencies, spurring growth for Ethereum, Ripple, Litecoin, and other currencies. In recent downturns for Bitcoin, however, the other virtual currencies have mirrored the downward trend of the leading virtual coin, as cash leaving Bitcoin has been invested in other assets.

With current developments, it is then imperative for you, as the investor, to not only look at Ripple's movement, but also to monitor the overall cryptocurrency market as all the signs indicate towards trends affecting *all* digital currencies, rather than just isolated pockets of upward or downward trajectories.

What does the future of cryptocurrency, as a general sector, look like? In the next chapter, predictions, forecasts, and other important considerations regarding the overall health of cryptocurrency will be taken up.

Chapter Summary

- Ripple continues to woo major financial institutions to its platform, counting MoneyGram and American Express among the major adopters of Ripple from 2017.
- XRP is now listed in over 50 international cryptocurrency exchanges, from only six listings at the start of 2017, indicating increasing demand.
- RippleNet, the blockchain network dedicated to enterprise users, now counts over 100 big financial service providers from different countries.

- Ripple was able to solve a problem that traditional payment solutions, such as SWIFT, were unable to correct, which is the transaction time for cross-border payments.

While Ripple has managed to carve its own niche in the cryptocurrency market, it is not immune to the upheavals of the sector in general, especially over the last few weeks.

Chapter Seven: The Future Of Cryptocurrency

What the cryptocurrency sector of the financial world will look like in ten years is not a hundred percent certain as of yet, although few will argue that digital currencies such as Ripple, Ether, Litecoin, Monero, and Bitcoin will have to remain pliable and open to change in order to stay relevant. The current state of cryptocurrency alone is already quite remarkable. Who would have thought that this concept would become not only a reality but the center of the digital money revolution in such a short time?

Bitcoin Brand Will Still Rule

For the immediate future, what does seem apparent is that while Ripple and the other digital currencies seem poised for growth, the Bitcoin brand will remain the most popular among investors, especially because Bitcoin has already established itself as the standard for peer-to-peer online currency technology in a decentralized platform. With the functions of transaction processing and verification, as well as issuance of new currency still decentralized among its community, Bitcoin will remain the standard by which other cryptocurrencies are measured.

This decentralized nature of Bitcoin will also spell the difference, in the near future, as the community of users will determine its very mechanism. Since there is no central authority overseeing Bitcoin's processes, and no government is backing the value of the cryptocurrency, the value or price of each Bitcoin depends fully on what investors are currently willing to pay for it. This could be either a boon or bane for the entire cryptocurrency sector, as recent developments have shown that Bitcoin wields much influence on how the rest of the cryptocurrencies, such as Ripple, are perceived in the market.

Increased Oversight On The Way

There are calls to increase the monitoring, or allowed oversight, of cryptocurrencies in various territories all over the world. This is due to the proliferation of illegal activities in the digital currency world, mainly because of the anonymity and decentralized nature of the platforms. Regulatory agencies and governments have been pushing for more rules that could curb the use of cryptocurrencies for illegal activities, but many also see this as a threat to the very nature of cryptocurrencies as alternatives to mainstream financial institutions.

What has been one of the biggest attractions for cryptocurrency is how it allows greater access to financial products. Cryptocurrency is not a slave to exchange rates, state restrictions, prevailing interest rates, and other policies set forth by central banks and governing authorities. As such, cryptocurrency can be enhanced as a universally acceptable form of payment and provide for faster, more convenient transactions particularly for users who need to transact with other users across the globe. Increased government scrutiny, however, could render these other advantages useless.

Attempts to curtail the freedom of cryptocurrency networks have been met with resistance also because they may curtail how digital money has democratized the process itself. A significant segment of today's population still does not have access to traditional financial services provided by banks and other financial providers. This is caused by various reason such as geographic limitations, lack of infrastructure, or the prohibitive costs usually tacked on to banking services especially in developing markets. What cryptocurrency has done is open up a new, digital global currency to these billions of individuals (unbanked population estimates numbers between 1.5 billion to 2 billion worldwide) by giving them access to peer-to-peer financial transactions, while bypassing the need for an established bank account or line of credit.

Will the democratized access to cryptocurrencies such as Ripple become unnecessarily restricted once governments step in and attempt to exercise control over these platforms? Worries regarding this potential scenario have caused jitters across the cryptocurrency from time to time, especially as territories announce moves to step in and interfere or limit how users are able to integrate cryptocurrencies into their daily lives.

For instance, in March of 2013, the Financial Crimes Enforcement Network released policies that defined virtual currency exchanges (where cryptocurrencies such as Ripple may be traded or stored) and their administrating entities as money service businesses. This new policy places digital currency exchanges under government regulation and gives the state more power to interfere in how users freely exchange digital cash.

Money laundering laws were also brought up in separate incidents in 2013, when the Department of Homeland Security froze an account of Bitcoin exchange MtGox at Wells Fargo Bank because of allegations of violating anti-money laundering laws. Also, the New York Department of Financial Services issued a number of subpoenas to 22 different virtual payment companies asking them to detail their current measures on how to protect consumers and also prevent instances of money laundering.

While money laundering and other illegal activities are a definite concern for consumers, there is clear disagreement about plans to increase the government's role in interfering with the activities of digital currency platforms. The thinking that prevails over the majority of those interested in virtual currencies today, highlights independence and increased control over personal affairs and transactions in everyday life. This is where cryptocurrency has strategically positioned itself, as it offers a level of security and privacy currently surpassing that of the oversight in banks, and with digital access that goes far beyond paper bills or coins. It is mirroring the continued transition of many aspects of daily life from the physical to the digital. Attempts to curtail the freedom of cryptocurrency platforms could mean a completely different reality for virtual money.

That is not to say, of course, that all forms of regulation would be necessarily bad. Sensible, responsible, and well-informed oversight may actually be beneficial to cryptocurrencies, not only for their existing stakeholders but also to further improve the perception of digital money as a viable form of investment. Regulation would be beneficial, for instance, in the speculative arena of Initial Coin Offerings or ICO's. ICO's have become the subject of intense scrutiny because of highly questionable practices of some entrepreneurs, and even cryptocurrency purists agree that government regulation for ICO's is not a bad thing.

Recently, the Securities and Exchange Commission of the United States has started to move towards regulation of ICO's, with the argument that some of these crypto assets and digital currencies are considered securities, and therefore fall under its regulation. The SEC, however, was careful not to make it seem that the agency was ready to stifle the growth of the cryptocurrency sector, as SEC Chairman Jay Clayton himself acknowledged that ICO's "…can be effective ways for entrepreneurs and others to raise funding, including for innovative projects."

Changing Perceptions

What is promising is that general perceptions on cryptocurrency in general are also changing. While there is a wariness that still exists regarding its potential for being used in illegal online activities, owing to the initial widespread use of digital currencies (Monero, in particular) in the dark web for trading questionable goods, much of the attention has now turned to the positive effects of cryptocurrency on new enterprises, developing economies, and emerging sectors of the market that can use cryptocurrency's peer-to-peer technologies and self-sustaining application to speed up development at much lower costs.

Ripple, in particular, is being hailed by financial institutions as a definite game-changer owing to its reliability, security, and speed. Transactions that used to take days to verify and process can now happen in real time, saving costs for all involved. Also, at the forefront is Ethereum with its smart contracts and decentralized applications that democratize the hierarchy and open up avenues for developers to continually contribute to the ever-changing face of the digital revolution. As these developments continue unabated, a more positive view of cryptocurrency also emerges even among those who initially held unfavorable notions on virtual money.

Is It A Bubble Waiting To Burst?

The fears regarding cryptocurrency now turn to concerns that it could be a bubble waiting to burst. Investors may be flocking to Bitcoin, Ethereum, Ripple, Litecoin, and other virtual currencies because of their continued media attention and their potential to become financially rewarding investments, but what if a sudden shake-up occurs and prices spiral downward? Fears of a bubble continue to hound cryptocurrencies each time Bitcoin and other digital currencies decline in market price.

As the market normalizes and price corrections naturally occur, however, we may see less of the volatility that has characterized the cryptocurrency sector, to be replaced by the optimism that much of this new technology is opening up new opportunities in the modern age. Blockchain technology and peer-to-peer virtual currencies have shown a remarkable resiliency, and have been able to bounce back from sudden market shocks and regain their footing despite the sell-offs.

In order for cryptocurrency platforms to minimize fears and highlight achievements, communities must turn their attention towards feasible solutions to address concerns regarding online security, such as hacking, malware, or ransomware. Blockchain platforms must introduce or experiment with methods that increase the privacy and security of users, as well as utilize more identification verification procedures without sacrificing the democratized and decentralized nature of cryptocurrency.

Merging Old And New

What Ripple has been able to achieve successfully is merging the emerging technology of blockchain with the established financial structures of big banks and corporate entities servicing the financial needs of consumers. Die-hard cryptocurrency analysts may balk at the idea of a digital currency working very closely with financial institutions seen as part of the establishment, but what should be recognized is the need to find a healthy, working compromise between both sides in order to move forward in a more efficient and secure path that benefits all stakeholders.

Fiat Cryptocurrencies Soon

Another trend that will shape the future of cryptocurrency is its adoption by more countries. Many countries around the world have already taken steps towards adopting cryptocurrency and reducing their dependence on the US dollar and other fiat currencies. Digital currencies may be at the center of more experimentation by governments as viable alternatives or replacements to paper currency, especially as cryptocurrencies move towards more stability.

The possibility of fiat cryptocurrencies, or state-backed digital currencies, have been floated around for a few years now. One of the earliest proponents of this idea was Mark Carney, Governor of the Bank of England. In 2016, in the wake of Brexit and concerns that the United Kingdom may be headed for recession and even depression, as well as the potential loss of London's standing as a financial capital of the world, Carney needed to calm the public's fears. He was also looking for ways to keep the economy running and initiate entrepreneurship despite the transition.

In the midst of the anxiety, Carney gave a speech at the Mansion House which was then published by the Bank of England. Carney gave a detailed vision that centered around blockchain and virtual currencies, and how these emerging technologies could pave the way for positive changes to the economy of the UK, not to mention the global financial hierarchy. He postulated that fintech may usher in a financial system that is more inclusive, and make the population of the world more informed, empowered, and connected to each other.

Carney's speech also gave the details of a digital currency project being started by the central bank, as the bank wanted to see how a state-backed cryptocurrency or "Britcoin" could potentially hedge the country's economy against major political upheavals such as Brexit. The project also aimed to explore ways that a fiat cryptocurrency could help in preventing or solving financial crimes, boost domestic competition, encourage innovative ideas, and foster the inclusion of more citizens.

According to another publication by the Bank of England in 2016, switching 30% of the country's current paper currency into a digital currency would increase GDP up to 3%, while also helping the central bank to maintain the stability of the business atmosphere. A similar pilot project on digital currency and blockchain technology had also been spearheaded by the Bank of Canada prior to Carney's speech.

As of 2017, some countries that have expressed interest or started projects on state-backed digital currencies include Russia, China, Dubai, and Venezuela. This 2018, initiatives regarding fiat cryptocurrencies are planned or expected in Singapore, Switzerland, South Korea, Japan, India, and Estonia. While some fiat cryptocurrencies are little more than government attempts to compete with existing cryptocurrencies, other countries are genuinely looking at the possibility of someday switching to digital currency.

This possibility again raises many opportunities for Ripple and its counterparts in virtual currency. If Ripple can establish itself as the leader in payment settlements and real-time transfers in the business sector, a partnership with a state-backed or fiat cryptocurrency would not only provide it with a tremendous boost in investor confidence and overall market perception, but also open the doors for revenue and potential rewards for existing Ripple investors and users.

Blockchain Revolutionizes Processes

In particular, governments around the world are recognizing the vast potential of the blockchain technology in improving services, streamlining operations, and providing a quicker and more organized standard in delivering vital information or essential transactions, all at more manageable costs. Blockchain is here to stay, and it is now up to governments and state agencies to figure out how to take advantage of this technology in the same way much of the corporate and financial industries have already benefitted from it.

Other industries will also wake up and see the vast potential of blockchain technology in improving their operations. According to the Blockchain Research Institute, major industries that can benefit from blockchain technology include retail and consumer goods, telecommunications, mass media, technology, health care, education, energy, manufacturing, and resources. In fact, big entities within these industries have already started pilot programs or implemented sweeping changes around blockchain technology, and this positive transformation around blockchain will inevitably lead to a greater understanding and acceptance of virtual currency as well.

Speaking of businesses, another trend to watch for in the cryptocurrency scene is how legacy companies and large retailers will jump in and accept Ripple, Bitcoin, Litecoin, Ether, and other popular virtual currencies for payment acceptance. As more and more users make the switch to cryptocurrency, merchants will see this as another way to maintain their market share and offer another option to consumers. Businesses that open up to cryptocurrency payment options will be seen as more willing to go with the times and join the revolution, while those who stubbornly refuse may find themselves in a conundrum to maintain a relationship with the digitally-savvy millennial market.

Cryptocurrency platforms, as a response, must ensure that they offer enticing deals and opportunities for merchants and retailers who express interest in accepting virtual cash payment options. With big-name companies warming up to the idea of accepting cryptocurrencies in their digital and physical storefronts, virtual currency protocols must be configured to allow immediate liquidation to fiat currencies as well, in order to maintain market volume.

What About Their Value?

As an interested investor in Ripple and cryptocurrency as a whole, you would of course want to know if the value of the market will continue to grow. Sure, the value of these currencies has risen over the years, experienced price drops, and then gone back up over time. But will the trend continue? Experts do see the market continuing to grow overall in value.

The cryptocurrency trend is still in the very early stages, and any trends in price changes we have seen so far are just the tip of the iceberg. Despite many industry watchers predicting a big crash in the cryptocurrency market, it has remained strong and managed to bounce back in the midst of volatility. The coming years are expected to be full of continued institutional buying of cryptocurrencies, and as an asset class, virtual cash will be hard to ignore for even the most traditional investors.

As already mentioned in previous chapters, in order to sustain this growth, virtual currency platforms will have to continue introducing innovation and injecting new ideas into the financial processes that consumers have come to know over the years. Ripple, for instance, will likely continue to see its XRP value rise in correlation to more partnerships and integrations with established finance companies. To the average investor, a company such as Ripple that gains the trust of banks and multinational companies with huge assets to protect means trustworthiness and reliability. After all, an international bank with much to lose will not dare risk its portfolio on an emerging technology with a shaky foundation.

Virtual Money And The Environment

Not to be neglected is the positive impact of cryptocurrency and blockchain technology in another area that ranks quite high in importance in society today -- environmental sustainability. There has been much criticism about how Bitcoin and other cryptocurrencies are driving up energy consumption particularly because of the constant need to mine currencies using computer processors. However, the mining requirement does not apply to all cryptocurrencies, and the environment-friendly effects of blockchain and cryptocurrencies outweigh the energy consumption.

Digital currencies, blockchain technologies, smart contracts, and wireless protocol all reduce or eliminate the need for paperwork, so this helps towards the goal of a global green economy. Virtual currencies also speed up transaction times at lesser costs, and often circumvent the need to consume more energy or fuel. With Ripple, for instance, instead of a sender having to consume fuel to drive to a local bank to transfer funds to the receiver, and then have to fill out information printed on paper, everything can be done electronically, saving time, fuel, and resource.

Blockchain technology maximizes available resources and reduces infrastructure and supply chains, thus saving resources and allowing organizations to channel the financial savings towards other environmentally-sustainable investments.

Obstacles Make Cryptocurrency Stronger

As the community of cryptocurrency continues to grow, so will the attacks and attempts to hack into their systems and steal assets. But as has been seen constantly, these attacks will serve to identify flaws or weak points in the security infrastructure of virtual currency protocols, and solutions will be implemented, rendering cryptocurrencies more resilient technologies. As Ripple and other cryptocurrencies experience more attempted attacks, security is beefed up and measures improve in the long run.

The upheavals, sell-offs, price fluctuations, and massive changes being experienced by the cryptocurrency sector may be likened to the growth of the World Wide Web in the 1990s. As more and more people were able to access the Internet, and personal computers became common, thousands of dot-com companies and IT firms sprouted up, all eager to cash in on the Internet revolution and become part of the growing trend. As the dot-com bubble burst, many naysayers proclaimed the end of Silicon Valley. But out of the dot-com crash emerged firms that were able to weather the crisis and grow to become even more resilient, with many still existing and in excellent shape today.

Critics of cryptocurrency will be around and will not cease, and discussions will continue to rage on both sides of the aisle. Virtual currencies, however, are here to stay. Proof of this is the adoption of the concept of peer-to-peer digital currencies by many big-name companies, banks, and even government agencies. With digital money and blockchain technology becoming more widespread, the industry as a whole will continue to go through its growth pains. This is necessary for cryptocurrencies to mature and become more prepared for the future.

As an interested investor in Ripple and cryptocurrency in general, what are some helpful tips you should keep in mind? We will take a look at some valuable insights in the next chapter.

Chapter Summary

- In order to survive the future, cryptocurrencies such as Ripple should be open to change and continue to innovate.
- Bitcoin remains to be the main marker for the cryptocurrency market, but growth will continue in the other virtual currencies.
- Efforts to increase oversight on cryptocurrencies are being met with both scepticism and concern among user communities.
- Some government agencies have been attempting to regulate other aspects of the crypto asset industry such as Initial Coin Offerings (ICO's) which are highly speculative.

- More major retailers and merchants will be accepting cryptocurrencies as payment options, giving consumers more choices.
- Volatility in the cryptocurrency market may become less as the market starts to normalize, and as blockchain technology continues to show resilience.
- Ripple has been successful at combining both established and emerging technologies into more efficient and streamlined protocols.
- Fiat cryptocurrencies are seen to be a trend in the coming years as governments see how virtual money can hedge states against economic upheavals.
- Blockchain technology is seen to be more widespread in industries such as retail, media, telecommunications, health care, education, technology, manufacturing, energy, and others.
- As Ripple integrates with more financial institutions, XRP's value will also tend to rise as more investors see it as a good investment.
- There will be increased awareness on environment sustainability and how cryptocurrency and blockchain can help towards a green economy.

The growing pains of cryptocurrency now may be likened to the early days of the Internet in the 90s leading up to the dot-com burst in 2001. Some fell by the wayside, but others grew stronger and emerged as winners.

Chapter Eight: Advice For Investing In Ripple

Choosing to invest in Ripple is not vastly different from any other investment decisions you will make. Whether this is the first time you are testing the waters of crypto asset investment, or you already have assets in other virtual currency platforms and would like to test Ripple out as well, your goal is to make informed decisions and also strategically position yourself to earn big in the long term.

Decide If You Are An Investor Or Saver

Before you part with your hard-earned money and pour your savings into Ripple, you first must establish whether you will be an active investor or a saver. These are two different concepts that you must understand, and in the real world, a combination of both may also be needed to keep yourself diversified enough while taking advantage of opportunities.

To the average person, there may be little difference between savings and investments; but saving and investing entail different strategies, and knowing these strategies can not only give you a better grasp of your financial situation while helping you attain more with your financial resources, fully seeing them utilized to your advantage.

Saving money means setting it aside for future use, whether planned or unplanned. As a usual example, when you sit down and take note of your monthly income and expenditures, it is highly suggested that you set aside a considerable portion of your income for emergencies, or a big purchase you are planning in the near future, perhaps even upcoming vacations or house repairs.

In traditional banks, various products and services are offered with the purpose of helping consumers to build their savings. These include savings accounts, certificates of deposit, time deposits, or safety vaults. Savings are usually designed to be relatively easy to access so the consumer has an additional pool of money to dip into in case an emergency expense comes up. Savings products and services usually also are insured by the financial institution, and incur a low interest rate.

Many people also opt to have their own type of savings, for instance, a safe or drawer in their home where they always keep cash on hand, or even coin banks for the children. The advantage to this form of saving is easier access to your cash when you need it; but because this is not held for safekeeping by a banking institution, it does not accrue any interest over time, and is not protected from theft or natural calamities.

In the context of Ripple, you may choose to purchase Ripple and store it away for long periods of time. As discussed in a previous chapter, it is recommended that your XRPs be stored in either a hardware wallet (most recommended because of its offline storage), or a web wallet. As you keep your XRP keys stored, their value rises or falls depending on prevailing market price.

Meanwhile, investing your money means utilizing it to fund various products, programs, and services that are created to earn higher returns over a longer period of time. Well-known types of investments in the traditional financial industry include stocks, mutual funds, securities, bonds, and other products consisting of the broader financial industry of borrowing and lending. As an investor, you consent to have your money be used by investment firms towards different transactions and investments of their own, and as a reward your money yields a much higher rate of profit than the usual savings account. The risk is also higher, so you stand to lose your investment if the stocks or bonds do not perform as expected.

Business entrepreneurship is also considered a form of investment. If you have a business concept, perhaps with a product or service to offer, or are partnering with a colleague or group to start up a company, you are investing your money in a potentially rewarding enterprise. A business which grows and achieves success may lead to your financial independence, allowing you to have a source of income that is comparable, if not higher, than if you were employed full-time for someone else; on the other hand, there is also a much higher risk of losing your investment if the business enterprise does not succeed.

In the context of Ripple, you may consider yourself an investor if your goal is to purchase XRPs, wait for an opportune time to sell them off when the price is higher, earn profits, and then repeat the process or invest in another crypto asset. The process of trading XRPs has not become as widespread as in other cryptocurrencies just yet, but with XRP's value rising dramatically, you should see more investors actively trading XRP units in order to earn big.

So, do you consider yourself a saver, or more of an investor? Most financial experts and planners would recommend a balance of both as the best way to manage your financial resources and diversify your options.

You may liken a cryptocurrency investment to investing in commodities. Commodities are assets such as base metals, precious metals, and other elements used in various industries. Commodities are invested in by traders via open market exchanges. In a similar way, cryptocurrencies are being used to fund financial applications or services, but investors also invest in them actively.

Consider Real World Usage

When considering your Ripple investment, you would want to look at the market capitalization and trade volume, as these are indicators of how much the virtual currency is actually being used in real world transactions. If you note the upward surge in the price of XRP just over the last 12 months alone, and how it has found its way near the top of the market capitalization rankings for cryptocurrencies, it is safe to say that Ripple is for real and is more than just a digital concept. It is being used, and is worth investing into.

Apart from the market capitalization of Ripple, you should also consider the collective volume of the cryptocurrency market to date, which exceeds the volume and market capitalization of many large multinational companies or corporations that have been around for many decades. This reflects growing usage and increasingly widespread acceptance of cryptocurrencies in general, so investing would be logical.

Room For Growth

Another consideration is the potential for growth and increased awareness in the overall cryptocurrency sector. Despite the massive gains already posted by Bitcoin, Ripple, and other virtual currencies, most people are still either slightly familiar with cryptocurrency or understand its concept. In the United States, only about 2 percent of Americans are using cryptocurrency.

What does this mean for you as a potential investor? There is much room for growth in Ripple and other digital currencies. If you think the state of the segment now is remarkable, consider where it will be in a few years' time as more people join the trend, thus increasing its trade volume and market price. This is why timing is very important in this type of investment. You would want to place yourself in a strategic position where you stand to profit big later on.

Cryptocurrency Must Solve An Existing Problem

One very important insight to remember as a cryptocurrency investor is to choose one that is actively involved in finding a solution to a common problem. The cryptocurrency you invest in must have a purpose to its existence and be seen as a catalyst for change or a solution to a problem, instead of just being a virtual currency that may deliver investment returns later on. There is nothing wrong with investing in a potentially financially rewarding product, of course. But in the evolving landscape of cryptocurrencies, you are more poised for long-term sustainability if your platform has evolved into a solution.

Knowing this, Ripple comes to mind as a definite solution to a problem. Before Ripple came about, there was a definite problem with payment settlements and cross-border transfers taking long periods of time to verify and approve. Transaction fees were prohibitive. Then, Ripple came up with a solution for a faster, cheaper, more stable payment protocol, along with a native asset, XRP, that could better facilitate transfers.

In time, Ripple has evolved into a solutions provider for financial institutions, raising its standing among its peers and increasing its importance to the mainstream financial industry. Still, its XRP native asset benefitted and also steadily became a lucrative investment. What we see, then, is Ripple as a virtual currency and real-time payments provider firmly taking root and raising its value to investors and users, thus making it more resilient to any possible changes in its segment.

Beyond Ripple, this is also why you would want to consider cryptocurrencies which are actively seeking to enter emerging or underdeveloped markets. Unlike in highly developed countries where banking and financial services are commonplace, there is still much room for improvement in services and infrastructure in developing societies. Traditional banking facilities are often lacking or completely non-existent, or prohibitive in cost in relation to the market being served.

In scenarios like this, cryptocurrencies have the vast potential to take over and capture the market. With less infrastructure and overhead costs needed to initiate and operate a virtual currency platform, digital money can provide what the banking institutions are unable to. This solves a problem, makes the cryptocurrency platform a part of the solution, and makes it a viable long-term investment option.

While there are definitely certain risks involved in investing your money in different financial products, services, and other types of investments, including cryptocurrencies, the potential layer of monetary success and stability afforded to your present and future security far outweigh the risks. This is especially true for cryptocurrencies such as Ripple. The best time to invest may be now, while the market is growing and has not reached complete saturation point yet.

There Is An Urgency

Perhaps what many people fail to see is the urgency of investing money now, especially if you are in a fairly stable enough position to do so. The younger in life you start to make investments, the less risk is associated, and the greater your chances as well of recouping any losses that may occur. For example, a young professional between 24 to 26 years of age who invests in stocks or mutual funds not only has the luxury of having more years ahead of him to watch the funds grow, but also more years to be able to gain back any money lost if the investment goes south.

The right cryptocurrency investments could provide you with a stable source of primary or secondary income, and for many people this is a dream that might seem unrealizable if present employment and income earnings are the only parameters. What investment does is maximize the assets and resources that you currently have by giving you the opportunity to grow them at a much faster and exponential rate than traditional savings options. A well-strategized portfolio of various investments managed and maintained over a significant period of time could lead to a healthy, stable financial standing for you and your family in the future, allowing you to not only enjoy a higher standard of living, but possibly also the luxury of not having to work as long and hard, and instead enjoy the fruits of your labor.

Investments also provide a form of financial security and fall back in case you run into unforeseen difficulties or emergencies. Most types of investment products and policies can provide liquidity and a source of funds if the need arises. While they are not as liquid or accessible as savings accounts or cash deposits, they are still a viable financial security blanket that can provide you additional leeway in case of a sudden upheaval in your situation. For cryptocurrencies such as Ripple, of course, funds are always available to you. Your investment or savings can be tapped for emergency use.

Because most investments are designed for long-term rewards, these products and services are one of the best ways to prepare for your retirement years. Whether you are fully aware of it or not, you will not have all your life to work and earn money. There will come a time when you will be too old to work, and the reality is the income derived from government benefits may not always be enough, or may not leave you enough for other pleasures, such as travelling or other personal pursuits. However, if you have had the foresight of making investments with significant rewards, your retirement years will be more comfortable, and you will be in a much better position to enjoy your labor.

Whatever your perspective or goals may be in Ripple investing, the potential for financial freedom and security is the underlying advantage of investments in cryptocurrencies. While the industry itself has been subject to much scrutiny and distrust because of abuses and mismanagement, the negative side of the crypto asset market should not take away from the positive reality and the opportunity to attain financial stability.

When Unsure, Ask

Financial professionals, counsellors, and planners may be able to assist you in understanding the ins and outs of the cryptocurrency market and how you can maximize the value and longevity of your investments. If you are unsure how to get started or do not understand all the basic concepts, there is nothing wrong with seeking assistance.

The truth is not everyone is well-versed with financial terms and concepts, and the guidance and mentoring of a financial professional may be what you need to really understand how cryptocurrency works and how you can benefit from it. It is not wrong to ask for help if you need it; in fact, it would be a costly mistake to not ask for assistance if you really have no idea how to go about with your investment path.

You can also make a self-assessment and see if the expertise of a financial planner is needed in your circumstance. If you have a working knowledge of the cryptocurrency market and how investments work, and you enjoy reading all about how this segment of the financial sector is growing in importance, perhaps a more hands-on approach to your investment efforts would be better suited for your needs, and the services of a financial professional may not be necessary in your case. You may still want to schedule a consultation from time to time with a professional financial planner who can update you on how to best maximize your investments, but otherwise, if you have the time and effort to commit to it, you may be better off taking care of matters on your own.

More importantly, finding the right financial professional is key to further strengthening and growing your investment. Financial advisors and planners are a dime a dozen these days; choosing the best one for you may be overwhelming. It is best to start your search within professional organizations, or referrals from a certified public accountant or a lawyer you know personally. Also, if you have family or friends who have cryptocurrency investments of their own and seem to have found some success with them, you may be able to ask for referrals from them also.

Educate Yourself Financially

Even if you have the professional expertise and know-how of a financial adviser or planner, it is still to your advantage to arm yourself with financial knowledge and investment strategies, especially in the ever-expanding and rapidly evolving world of cryptocurrency. Financial literacy not only makes you more aware of the goings-on in the world of finances, but also makes you more equipped to get a better handle on your personal finances, eventually leading to financial freedom.

Seminars, classes, and courses related to various aspects of the financial industry are usually offered at local community or junior colleges, or in libraries and other non-profit organizations. Check for classes and seminars in your locality; many are offered free of charge or at minimal costs. Also, take advantage of any literature, books, and reading materials and resources that you can get your hands on to further expand your knowledge of the investment world. You will also benefit from making comparisons to how traditional financial services work compared to the cutting-edge concepts being introduced by virtual currency platforms.

As you become more familiar with Ripple and its counterparts in the world of cryptocurrency, you will realize just how much there is to learn and to understand. At times it can be overwhelming especially as you become more involved in the process and see just how technical and data-intensive the Ripple protocol can be. Remember to be patient with yourself and to trust the process. Take it one step at a time. Try not to overload yourself with information, but instead let your mind absorb the concepts at a comfortable and appropriate pace.

Chapter Summary

- In the world of Ripple, you may opt to save your XRPs and monitor the market, or become an active investor engaged in trading currency.
- The trade volume and market capitalization of Ripple indicate that it is being used in the real world.
- The cryptocurrency market has so much room to grow because most people have not fully embraced its concepts yet.
- For long-term success, a cryptocurrency such as Ripple must be involved in problem solving.
- Urgency and timing are important considerations in Ripple investing.
- Financial planners and experts are great sources of additional information regarding cryptocurrency.
- You should arm yourself with as much knowledge by reading and researching on the topic.

Final Words

Some people think it is already too late to jump into the cryptocurrency trend and start investing, citing the high price of many of the leading virtual coins which may prohibit new investors from joining in. On the other hand, there are those who believe that the cryptocurrency market is still in its infancy and should not be regarded yet as a good investment because of its wild fluctuations and frequent volatility.

But when do you take action and start learning and finding your own place in the world of cryptocurrencies? Ripple is continuing a rapid time of growth and development that has not only attracted investors but also interested partners who are seeing the potential of what Ripple can offer to their own structures. The most opportune time, indeed, may be somewhere between an idea's initial foray into the consciousness of its market, and well before it peaks and reaches saturation point.

As you consider Ripple and whether investing in this virtual currency is right for you, be mindful of what is happening in the blockchain and peer-to-peer digital currency sector. Developments are occurring every day, to be discussed in detail by pundits and experts in financial news channels and webinars. The future, as they say, is upon us today. With the rise of cryptocurrency, the world is moving rapidly towards a fully digital and cashless society, one that may or may not be fiat-based, but would very likely be in digital form somehow.

How should you take this trend? Just like any other investment, you must avoid getting too hyped in the moment and making rash, ill-informed decisions, but on the other hand, it is also not good to stay too close to the shore and miss out on all the action waiting out there. The world of Ripple is highly active and offers much potential for the investor who has the guts to wade out into the deep end of the water and figure out the workings of blockchain and virtual cash for himself.

There is no book, resource, or speaker that can fully communicate the concept of cryptocurrency investing and future potential better than first-hand experience. Sometimes, you just have to see for yourself, live through the moment, and come to your own realization regarding this currency that has been dubbed as the future of money. Who would not want to have a sneak peek into the future, after all? With Ripple, you get the chance to test for yourself how the financial service industry will look like years from now.

Years from now, you will look back fondly and remember those times when inter-bank transactions or wire transfers could take a few days to clear, and realize that at the precipice of the revolution, when it all started changing, you were right there in the middle of it all, experiencing the revolution that was initiated by this payment solutions provider utilizing blockchain to make transactions real time. Long wait times and exorbitant transaction fees will become mementos of the not-too-distant past.

Where will the cryptocurrency trend take us? For now, what is apparent is how things are shaking up and being transformed to their very core by the rise of digital currency. Where exactly it all leads is anyone's guess, but if the dramatic explosion of cryptocurrencies within the last five years is any indication, it looks like a future that will challenge the norms and force all stakeholders to rethink how finance is done worldwide.

If you enjoyed this book, please take the time to leave me a review on Amazon. I appreciate your honest feedback, and it helps me to continue producing high-quality books.

Other Ikuya Takashima books available on Amazon

Cryptocurrency: How I Paid my 6 Figure Divorce Settlement by Cryptocurrency Investing, Cryptocurrency Trading

Ethereum: The Ultimate Guide to the World of Ethereum, Ethereum Mining, Ethereum Investing, Smart Contracts, Dapps and DAOs, Ether, Blockchain Technology

Blockchain: The Ultimate Guide To The World Of Blockchain Technology, Bitcoin, Ethereum, Cryptocurrency, Smart Contracts

Bitcoin: The Ultimate Guide to the World of Bitcoin, Bitcoin Mining, Bitcoin Investing, Blockchain Technology, Cryptocurrency

ICO: The Ultimate Guide To Investing In ICOs, ICO Investing, Initial Coin Offering, Cryptocurrency Investing, Investing In Cryptocurrrency

Litecoin: The Ultimate Guide to the World of Litecoin, Litecoin Crypocurrency, Litecoin Investing, Litecoin Mining, Litecoin Guide, Cryptocurrency

About The Author

31-year-old Ikuya Takashima is a Software Developer, entrepreneur, investor and author.

Ikuya first entered the world of Cryptocurrency in 2014 when he finally decided to invest in Bitcoin after several years of following the online currency. Ikuya is now a Cryptocurrency expert & enthusiast with an impressive Cryptocurrency portfolio and investments in several Bitcoin & Ethereum startups.

Ikuya's latest venture is to share his knowledge and passion on the world of Cryptocurrencies with the goal of making seemingly complex and intimidating topics simple and easy-to-read.

In Ikuya's spare time he likes to read, travel and spend time with family and friends.

Made in the USA
Lexington, KY
18 October 2018